WHY THE BISHOPS WENT TO VALDOSTA

An Essay
Based on
an Article by Dr. Randall Balmer

Dr. Ronald E. Cottle

Why the Bishops Went to Valdosta

REC Ministries
664 Sweetwater Drive
Cataula, GA 31804
www.roncottle.com

Special permission to use this article (In Deepest Georgia, a Pentecostal Congregation Goes High Church) has been granted by its author, Dr. Randall Balmer.

TABLE OF CONTENTS

TO: LIFE LEADERS EVERYWHERE

Here is a story that might surprise you — even shock you — on first reading. But I know it to be true and genuine. This is the church built by my oldest and dearest friend since third grade. He is Jimmy White, his older son is Stan (deceased in 2020), whom I knew well and admired. His younger son is Michael, Rector of America's oldest church, Christ Church (Episcopal) founded by John Wesley in 1733 and older than the nation (1776), in Savannah, Georgia.

This is another sign of what God is doing in this third millennium which some call the Biblical "Third Day." A Day of resurrection and power of the Spirit. I believe He is arousing His Church from its slumber and calling it back into its apostolic wholeness and oneness.

Even as He awakens and calls out His Remnant Ekklesia as a vanguard and instrument of restoration, He is also seeking to awaken His sleeping giant, His whole Church, for the inevitable Armageddon that Jesus predicted when He promised to build His Ekklesia (Matthew 16:18) that the Gates of Hades could not resist.

As you see from this article published in Christianity Today, leading Evangelical magazine, Stan's vision was a church that is fully charismatic (Holy Spirit lead), fully evangelical (Word-centered), and also fully liturgical and sacramental (open to worship in every way desirable by the people of the local ekklesia and not prohibited by the Word or the Spirit).

I visited Christ Church in Savannah where Michael is Rector (Senior Pastor) and experienced a service of worship. The hymns were uplifting and the liturgy 98% Scripture. The sermon was excellent by any measure and the Holy Communion an experience with Christ and His Body. I truly sensed the presence of the Lord in the worship.

Grasping a part of our assignment we have been missing.

While we are rightly focusing our energies on those outside the Church who have been turned away by its self-centeredness, dividedness, and exclusiveness, and at the same time on those in Pentecostal, Charismatic circles who are disillusioned and fed up with hero-worship, empire-building, and extravagance, we must not fail to turn our attention also to the millions of God's children within the institutional Church. These are God's people.

They are Christians who are saved and living for Christ. Some would say: "Okay, then leave them alone. Let the Church be what it is and let's build the Ekklesia with new blood by converting sinners outside the Church."

Ekklesia is a called-out remnant.

This would be a mistake of the greatest proportions! We must remember that Ekklesia is another word for Remnant in the Old Testament. The very idea behind Jesus' use of Ekklesia is the Old Testament Remnant. The Ekklesia is the Remnant of the Church. We are the Church. We are none other than the Church; we are not a separate entity alongside the Church. We are a Remnant of the Church called out and anointed to do what the Church is called to do but is not doing as it should.

The only difference between us and them is that we have the revelation of the Ekklesia (called-out ones on mission). We have caught a glimpse of God's Eternal Purpose for His Church and have begun to work toward it once again!

The Church is our mother, not our enemy! If there were no Church, there would be no Ekklesia. Let us not fight the Church; let us not "shoot our mother" just because we have a revelation from God that she does not have any longer. Instead, let us love her and find a way, God's way, to inculcate this revelation into her psyche as God has given it to us.

They already reverence Christ. They are already the Body of Christ. They do not need to be converted to Christ. They need to be reactivated to the mission of the Church, the Eternal Purpose of God. Yes, we must continue to preach the Gospel to those who have not heard. Yes, we must continue to win souls to Christ, as many as possible. We need always to do this. However, we must also love and arouse our brothers and sisters in Christ to the purpose of Christ and His Church in this season.

It is not His purpose to win a few or even many individuals to Christ and then snatch us away from the earth and burn it with His enemies in it. This is the "house lie" that Satan has perpetrated in the Church and gotten many Christians to believe. God wants all the earth back. To win all the cosmos for which Jesus died is God's Eternal Purpose. Every nation or people group worshipping Him in Christ in their own way with their own values, idiosyncrasies, mores, and social culture.

Our Father and Creator-God loves variety. Not one leaf is an exact replica of another, nor fish, nor fowl, let alone human beings or other living creatures. God does not want us all to worship Him in the exact same manner. He loves our individuality and our cultural variations. The grand vision of the Father is that we all become "a people" by choice of Him, Christ, and each other. Black, white, brown, yellow, all flowing together because of our love for His "Pattern Son" and each other as interdependent parts of one Body.

He is seeking to look upon earth once again and see His Son. However, not the incarnate, only begotten Son, but His corporate Son, His "many sons brought to glory" living together and loving each other, worshipping, and serving our one God with all our hearts as one people making His enemies His footstool and destroying the works of the devil.

This is the Kingdom of God manifested. This longing is already in us by His Spirit (Romans 8:19). However, when His Church, His people as one truly does His will upon earth, then His Kingdom will come into full glorious manifestation upon earth as it is in heaven. Then we will rule and reign with Him, our Lord Jesus, not only in the earth, but from there throughout all His renewed creation.

What God created in Genesis 1 -2 will be fulfilled as described in Revelation 21 – 22.

Then the seventh angel sounded: And there were loud voices in heaven, saying, "The kingdoms of this world (cosmos) have become the kingdoms of our Lord (Jesus) and of His Christ (anointed – the Church in all her glory as the Bride and co-regent of Christ), and He shall reign forever and ever!"

(Revelation 11:15)

As Handel put it: HALLELUJAH!

FOREWORD

This article, published on September 24, 1990, in the nation's leading evangelical magazine, was written by a professional writer, Dr. Randall Balmer, a professor of religion at Dartmouth College. He also wrote *Mine Eyes Have Seen the Glory: A Journey into the Evangelical Subculture in America.* After writing this piece, Professor Balmer later became an Episcopal priest. He has also served as an Episcopal parish rector.

These signs of unity or Biblical oneness in the Church are beginning to multiply. While the attempt to unite the Body of Christ on legal, liturgical, and governmental grounds known as the Ecumenical Movement failed, it did not fail because disunity is better, but because the means of attaining such unity were wrong.

It is the Spirit Who is the cause and reason for unity. The Bible says it simply: He that does not have the Spirit of Christ is none of His (see Romans 8:9b). It is the Holy Spirit within the members of the Body that alone is the unifying factor of His Church. This was true in the early Church, and it is still true today.

In this new millennium we have begun to see the emergence of the Church as a single spiritual entity and not just a group of organizations or institutions.

The brilliant young Stan White envisioned the Church as charismatic, operating in spiritual gifts and anointings, evangelical, based solely on the Word of God, the Evangel, for its direction and values, and liturgical – sacramental, worshipping in a free and open manner suited to the socio-cultural preferences of the local community of faith.

This is where the Church is going in the present secularism. Harvard Professor Dr. Harvey Cox indicates in his book, *The Future of Faith*, that we have entered the "Age of the Spirit." O, may we continue to walk out in faith a movement of the Holy Spirit that many of us sense today with the goal of making us one in Christ: Jew and Gentile, black and white, rich and poor, Liturgical and Pentecostal, Protestant and Catholic—all One in Christ.

Ephesians 2:14-16, 18

14 "For He Himself is our peace, who has made both one, and has broken down the middle wall of separation, 15 having abolished in His flesh the enmity, that is, the law of commandments contained in ordinances (dogmas), so as to create in Himself one new man from the two, thus making peace, 16 and that He might reconcile them both to God in one body through the cross, thereby putting to death the enmity (opposition, hatred)... 18 For through Him we both have access by one Spirit to the Father."

IN DEEPEST GEORGIA, A PENTECOSTAL CONGREGATION GOES HIGH CHURCH

CHRISTIANITY TODAY - SEPTEMBER 24, 1990 –

BY

DR. RANDALL BALMER

(SPECIAL PERMISSION TO USE THIS ARTICLE HAS BEEN GRANTED BY ITS AUTHOR)

In Valdosta, Georgia, a large billboard looms over North Valdosta Road, a winding highway on the outskirts of town. On a white background next to a bejeweled crown, tall, bold letters spell out: Church of the King. Beneath that, a smaller sign reads: Sunday 10:30 AM & 7:00PM/Thursday 7:00 PM—Stan J. White, Pastor.

The sign is tasteful and artistic, but it is also conspicuous, even from a distance—part of the Mail Pouch Tobacco genre of American roadside advertising that grabs you by the lapels and demands your attention.

Less than 100 feet away, in front of a parking lot and gray cinder-block warehouse, the same people responsible for the billboard have planted a much smaller sign. You have to walk close to see the fine print at the bottom, but it also reads Church of the King. Above that is a familiar shield set against a light blue-and-white background: The Episcopal Church Welcomes You.

Therein lies a story. The name emblazoned on the billboard belongs to a man in his late twenties with chiseled features and a slight frame. Stan White has dark hair and deep, brooding eyes, but they are not unfriendly. He carries a gentle and unprepossessing mien of seriousness about him; he is the fellow who asked too many questions in your high-school algebra class. He comes to the office during the week dressed casually; on Good Friday, for instance, he wore a meticulously starched, button-down shirt, designer denims, and boat shoes with white sweatsocks.

The prep-school attire, however, is misleading. Stan White has impeccable Pentecostal credentials and boasts that he is a fourth-generation Pentecostal preacher. "I'm very proud of my Pentecostal heritage," he insists. White's great-great uncle, a Missionary Baptist preacher, had a Pentecostal experience around 1908 and was kicked out of his denomination. He then joined the Assemblies of God when it was organized at Hot Springs, Arkansas, in 1914. White's grandfather and grandmother were also ordained in the Assemblies of God, as was his father, James White, a native of Columbus, Georgia. He served churches in southern California and Florida before returning to Georgia 25 years ago to take over a struggling Assemblies of God church in Valdosta. James, a handsome, white-haired gentleman known affectionately to his many devoted followers as "Brother Jimmy," guided Evangel Assembly of God from a handful of people in 1968 into one of Valdosta's largest congregations, with two weekly television broadcasts, a 1,500-seat auditorium, and approximately $3 million in assets.

In the early 1980s, Stan White, after two years at Valdosta State College and a data-processing job in Houston, felt called to the ministry. He joined the staff of his father's church as minister of music in 1982. In the ensuing years the elder White, edging toward retirement, asked his son to take on more and more of the pastoral duties at Evangel. About this time, in the mid-eighties, some extraordinary changes began to take place in Stan's life and, by extension, in Evangel Assembly of God.

"Evangel had always been a teaching church," White explains, and beginning in 1984 or thereabouts the church started to talk about what it meant to worship God. "I began to understand the importance of worship as more than just preaching followed by an altar call," he says. White still believed then, as he does now, in the "present reality of the Holy Spirit. That doesn't mean that we speak in tongues in our worship services. Rather, we believe in tongues as a personal devotional experience." The "present reality of the Holy Spirit" manifested itself at Evangel in lively and spontaneous services marked by outstretched arms, dancing, clapping, and shouting.

Despite the spirited worship, however, White sensed that something was missing from the services, and he grew increasingly uneasy with the altar calls that seemed to be directed week after week toward winning new converts rather than nurturing those already within the fold. White turned to church history. Growing up Pentecostal, he explains, he had little understanding of anything that had happened before the Azusa Street Pentecostal revivals in Los Angeles just after the turn of the century. While reading Irenaeus and other church fathers, White became convinced the early church had been both liturgical and sacramental, and that seemed to suggest that Pentecostalism, despite its insistence upon the gifts of the Spirit from the Acts of the Apostles, had not fully appropriated the richness of worship in the early church.

In Pentecostalism, White explains, the sacraments are called "ordinances," and Evangel Assembly of God observed the Lord's Supper once a month at most, and sometimes as infrequently as once a year. "We didn't treat it with any respect or dignity," he says.

In the midst of rethinking evangelical worship, White became seized with what he calls an "ecumenical spirit." He studied Roman Catholicism as well as Anglicanism, Lutheranism, and other liturgical traditions. A friend gave him a copy of the Episcopal Book of Common Prayer, which White began using in his private devotions. Most important, he attended a liturgical church and felt a spiritual quickening. "I experienced God there," White says, his voice still registering astonishment several years after the event. "That wasn't supposed to happen. It shocked me."

Somewhat tentatively, White shared some of his thinking with his family and congregation. He began to teach about church history, the creeds, and the sacraments. "We started incorporating some of those elements into our worship," he says, including a weekly celebration of the Lord's Supper. By 1987 Evangel Assembly of God in Valdosta, Georgia, was very likely the only Pentecostal church in the nation to open its services with a processional.

A large segment of the congregation greeted these changes with enthusiasm, others with curiosity, even bemusement. Still others were not so sure. On Thursday, August 11, 1988, the deacons called an emergency board meeting to remove Stan White as pastor. His father, James, who was semiretired by then and had built the church from virtually nothing, tendered his resignation as well.

"I thought at the time, 'It's over,'" Stan White recalls. If he still sounds a trifle defensive about the incident, he seems not at all bitter. "They said my theology was newfangled. They didn't realize that my theology was old."

At ten minutes of seven on Good Friday evening, 1990, a half-dozen automobiles and pickup trucks gathered in the parking lot of Church of the King, the warehouse on North Valdosta Road that once served as a boat showroom. A small group of people, ranging in age from midteens to midsixties, congregated outside the door. Each arrival set off another round of greeting and hugging. Nearly everyone carried two books: a Bible and a red-leather, deluxe edition of the Book of Common Prayer. The Bibles were worn and well-thumbed. The prayer books were new, the gilded edges barely disturbed. These were commemorative editions, for in two days, on Easter Sunday evening, these people, together with about 200 of their fellow congregants from Church of the King, would be confirmed in the Episcopal Church.

Although the conversation touched on other matters, it usually veered back to the events coming on Sunday night. "We're so excited, we can hardly stand it," one woman remarked before breaking into giddy laughter. "This is all still pretty new to us," a man explained, "but I think we're ready."

Ready or not, they had not come this far on impulse alone. After White's ouster from Evangel Assembly of God, a number of people from that congregation urged him to start his own church and continue combining Pentecostal worship with liturgical forms. White claims that beginning another church was the furthest thing from his mind; he had no intention of dividing Evangel Assembly of God even more than it already was. "We're not rebellious people," he insists. "We're not fighting people." The entreaties mounted, nevertheless, and, after consulting with his family and other members of his former congregation, he decided to relinquish his Assemblies of God credentials and announce a meeting for those who might be interested in forming a new church. Two-hundred-fifty showed for what became the first gathering of Church of the King. Starting a church from scratch, however, proved to be no easy task. "We didn't have so much as a paper clip," White says. The fledgling congregation met at two other locations—a furniture warehouse and the city auditorium—before moving to the warehouse on North Valdosta Road.

Intellectually, White kept moving as well. Although he maintains he was scrupulous about not violating Assemblies of God theology while at Evangel, the lack of denominational constraints at Church of the King afforded him freedom to experiment. The clergy started wearing vestments, the congregation repeated several creeds, and Church of the King celebrated the Lord's Supper every Sunday.

As the congregation approached its first anniversary in August 1989, White observed 40 days of fasting and prayer in order to seek guidance and direction for the church. It had been a good year, on balance, with strong and growing attendance, a number of outreach programs, and general satisfaction with the attempt to combine historic forms with charismatic fervor. Church of the King was also interracial, with African-Americans making up about 30 percent of its membership. "One of our real missions,"

White said, "has been to break down the walls of prejudice." White himself, however, was growing restless. "I wanted not merely to implement these historic creeds and practices, but also to identify with the historic church," he explains. "I suddenly had the sense that I was just bootlegging all this."

He initially resisted those sentiments; the one that followed was even more preposterous. "I felt my spirit drawn to the Episcopal Church, almost like a call," he said. White demurred at first, sure that his family, his pastoral staff, and certainly his congregation would not abide such a dramatic move. "I just didn't think they'd go for it," he says, "and even if they did, I was sure that the Episcopalians wouldn't go for it."

Finally, after a protracted inner struggle, White said, "Okay, God, I'll make some inquiries." He first floated the idea with an acquaintance, Jacoba Hurst, rector of Saint

Anne's Episcopal Church in Tifton, Georgia, who later confessed he was so astonished by White's overture "that I thought he had been under some stress." Hurst and White talked for five hours the next day, at the conclusion of which Hurst telephoned Harry W. Shipps, Episcopal bishop of Georgia. "There was a long silence at the other end of the phone," Hurst recalled, but he succeeded in setting up a meeting in which White's earnestness and sincerity won out over the bishop's initial skepticism.

White then had to confront his congregation. His voice timid and anxious, he asked permission to pursue affiliation with the Episcopal Church, careful to point out that it was a long process and that their efforts might be derailed at any one of several junctures. "The words were barely out of my mouth," White recounted, "before the entire congregation rose from its chairs in a standing ovation."

White had reason to be surprised. Most evangelicals generally look askance at Episcopalians because—well, because Episcopalians have frequently looked askance at them. The United States has no established religion in the sense of a state church, but no denomination in America is more identified with the establishment—those who control wealth and power—than the Episcopal Church. Of the nation's 41 Presidents, 12 have been Episcopalians. Twenty of the 100 U.S. Senators—one-fifth—are Episcopalians, a representation far out of proportion to the American population. For much of this century, on the other hand, evangelicals have felt themselves cut off from the corridors of wealth and power and influence. They feel awkward with the formalism and ceremony of high-church liturgy. "I'm always uncomfortable in an Episcopal church," a Methodist once remarked. "I feel like I'm at a fancy dinner party, and I'm never sure which fork to use."

Although charismatic renewal has had a profound influence in some Episcopal parishes, it is quite something else for the liturgical tradition to transform the worship of an entire Pentecostal congregation in the Deep South. The ancient divide between the formal and powerful, on the one hand, and the fervent and powerless, on the other, makes Church of the King all the more unusual. This is not a congregation consisting overwhelmingly of educated, professional, upwardly mobile evangelicals.

South-central Georgia has much to recommend it, with stands of pine trees alternating with grassy fields and peach trees in neat, carefully calibrated rows. This is Baptist country (I tried to tally the number of Baptist churches between Albany and Valdosta, but quickly lost count). Many of the restaurants in Valdosta will take a dollar off the price of your Sunday dinner if you can produce a bulletin as proof that you attended church that morning. Despite its undeniable charms, however, Valdosta, Georgia, hardly strikes a casual observer as the crossroads of culture, and that makes Church of the King's pilgrimage from Pentecostalism to Episcopalianism all the more extraordinary. "I envision a church that is fully charismatic, fully evangelical, but also fully liturgical and sacramental," White says. "We want to see all those elements working simultaneously."

Carolyn Dinkins, an affable, attractive woman in her forties, sets a bountiful table at her lakefront home outside Valdosta. She absented herself early from the Sunday morning service on Easter to complete preparations for the noon meal. Robert, her husband, stayed behind longer in order to socialize after the service and also, it seemed, to augment the guest list. Carolyn took it in stride.

When it was time to sit down to macaroni and cheese, string beans, squash, creamed corn, roast venison, country stuffed sausages, apple cobbler, and buttermilk biscuits with Georgia cane syrup, more than a dozen people had gathered, a congenial mixture of visitors and old friends. Ed and Jane Black had driven down from the Atlanta area to witness the day's events. Gordon and Blake Weisser, retirees from Houston, put Valdosta on their itinerary when they read about Church of the King in an Episcopal newsletter.

For Carolyn and Robert Dinkins, Ken and Rachel Reeves fall into the category of old friends. The Reeveses lived in Valdosta until recently; now they manage a trailer park in Dade City, Florida, but hope to move back to Georgia soon. Patricia and Bennett Thagard are farmers outside of Valdosta. Bennett, a rugged, burly man, possesses a ready smile and a bone-crushing handshake, both of which have assumed the status of legend among the congregants at Church of the King. "When people found out a few years ago that Bennett Thagard had become a Christian," Ann White, Stan's mother, explained on Friday evening, "they just couldn't believe it. 'Bennett Thagard?' they said. But let me tell you, the Lord just got ahold of him!"

The Sunday table conversation was abuzz with the historical significance of the confirmations that would take place that evening. The Prayers of the People at Church of the King that morning had included the petition that God would "do his thing tonight." Before dinner at the Dinkins home, the guests had gathered in the Dinkinses' spacious kitchen and held hands in a large circle while Robert Dinkins prayed. He had acknowledged before God "the momentous occasion" ahead and asked that "the Holy Spirit be there in all his power tonight."

After the prayer, Dinkins recounted his own spiritual pilgrimage. "I started attending Evangel Assembly of God in 1961," he said. "I used to be a segregationist 'til God turned me around." Dinkins recalled his initial misgivings about Stan White and White's movement toward high-church liturgy. "He made me so mad sometimes," he said, shaking his head; but the more Dinkins studied the Bible for himself, the more persuaded he became that White was on to something. "The Lord began to lead the congregation into uncharted areas as far as the Pentecostal movement is concerned."

The interior of Church of the King, the erstwhile boat showroom, has been tastefully decorated in cool colors. The steel beams supporting the roof are white, with long rows of fluorescent lights suspended from them. The cinder-block walls sport a fresh coat of paint the color of eggshells tinted ever so slightly with a lavender hue. The carpet is plush and purple, and the congregation sits on comfortable chairs upholstered in a gray tweed fabric.

The decor may be cool, but the Easter evening service was anything but cold. At 6:45 the music started, loud and lively and celebratory. The congregation rose spontaneously to its feet:

He's alive again.

The stone's been rolled away.

He's alive again.

He's no longer where He lay.

He's alive again,

I can hear the angels say,

"Let all the world rejoice, He's alive."

Gregg Kennard, the church's minister of music, directed the 50-voice choir accompanied by three trumpets, a violin, a flute, two clarinets, an electric bass guitar, and a percussion section (including timpani) behind the keyboard of a synthesizer.

By the time the orchestra segued into the next song, "Celebrate Jesus, Celebrate!" some hands were clapping, while others flailed the air. "Let's bless the Lord," Kennard shouted into his microphone. The congregation obliged with arms beating the air in ecstasy. Each song dissolved seamlessly into the next; the congregation appeared to know how to respond to each one. When the tempo picked up for "Sing Unto the Lord a New Song," the congregation quickened its pace and began dancing, a kind of quick, rhythmic hopping from one foot to the other, with arms swinging in a bouncy military swagger. Midway through the song, Church of the King looked more like Tuesday night aerobics class than Easter Sunday in an Episcopal parish.

Outside the sanctuary, crucifer, acolytes, dancers, thurifer (the one who carries the incense), clergy, and bishops fell into line during "How Magnificent Is Your Name, O Lord," a loud and stately march. The acolytes in their new red cassocks looked a bit unsteady, their eyes shifting furtively as they processed around the back of the auditorium and up the center aisle, leaving the sweet smell of incense in their wake. The visiting clergy, Episcopal priests from all over the diocese and from other dioceses as well, numbered two dozen. They processed just behind the pastoral staff and sat in a special section to the right of the altar. Four bishops wearing miters (traditional pointed hats thought to symbolize the tongues of flame that fell on the apostles at Pentecost) and dressed in their liturgical finery brought up the rear, followed by Bishop Shipps, a tall, bearded man walking with his crozier (shepherd's staff), the symbol of his office.

There had been an almost palpable air of excitement in the auditorium since five o'clock that afternoon. The processional itself symbolized the extraordinary character of the evening's events—the venerable medieval pageantry juxtaposed with loud and lively celebration—even as the music swelled toward a crescendo. With the cross and the banners in their stands, the clergy at their chairs, the dancers in repose, and the bishops at their stations, the singing finally reached a climax, whereupon the congregation—bishops and clergy included—broke into sustained and spontaneous applause.

Stan White stepped to the podium and savored the moment before leading another song of praise. One of the bishops and several of the visiting clergy had their arms outstretched, the traditional Pentecostal posture of praise to God and openness to the Holy Spirit. Only at the reading of the psalm, well into the service, did the congregation sit down. "Happy are they who have not walked in the counsel of the wicked," the congregation said in unison, "nor lingered in the way of sinners, nor sat in the seats of the scornful."

My eyes wandered to the contingent of clergy seated in the section adjacent to me. When Jacoba Hurst brought Stan White, this erstwhile Assemblies of God pastor, before the commission on ministry for the Diocese of Georgia, Hurst feared that he had ushered White into the seat of the scornful. "Some of these guys are rather hostile, dour clerics who don't suffer fools gladly," Hurst recalled. "They were reserved and cautious at first," he said; but then something extraordinary happened: "There was the presence of God in that room." He continued, "I couldn't speak. It was like some kind of revival."

The committee interrogated White at some length and then asked him to withdraw so they could deliberate. To his surprise, Hurst noticed that several members of the committee, these "hostile, dour clerics," were weeping. "I had a tremendous sense of destiny," he said about White's candidacy for ordination. "We felt that he was there by appointment from God. I really feel that he's been sent to the Episcopal Church."

John Howe, the bishop of Orlando, seemed to agree. When he strode to the podium to deliver the homily, he asked, "Are we having fun yet?" Judging by the congregation's enthusiastic response, the answer was yes. "This is a very exciting evening," he said. "This is something of historic proportions." Howe's sermon referred both to the archbishop of Canterbury, the spiritual head of the worldwide Anglican Communion, and Charles Parham, a Pentecostal preacher from Topeka, Kansas, who is generally regarded as the progenitor of Pentecostalism in America. Quoting a nineteenth-century Anglican churchman, Howe compared the Episcopal Church to a great, carved marble fireplace, and the spiritual ardor of nineteenth-century Methodists and twentieth-century Pentecostals to a fire. The fire, Howe declared, belongs in the fireplace. "We welcome this congregation of charismatic Christians into our church," he said, whereupon the bishops, the priests, and the congregation broke into applause. "Let the fire loose in the fireplace," he bellowed in conclusion. "Amen!"

After yet another song, this one punctuated with rhythmic clapping, White stepped to the podium and echoed the refrain. Presenting his congregation as candidates for confirmation in the Episcopal Church,

White addressed Bishop Shipps and said, "It's our desire to put the fire in the fireplace." The five bishops in all their splendor spread out in front of the altar. Then the congregation, numbering well over 200, formed a single queue in the center aisle, each person waiting for the next available bishop. Each bishop dabbed oil on the candidate's forehead, laid his hands on the candidate, and recited the form for confirmation from the Book of Common

Prayer: "Strengthen, O Lord, your servant Rachel with your Holy Spirit; empower her for your service; and sustain her all the days of her life. Amen." Each bishop, veteran of thousands of confirmations over the years, had his own style; one concluded each recitation with a smile and a light, playful slap on the cheek symbolizing that the Christian life would not be easy.

Many received their confirmations with outstretched arms. Not a few eyes were filled with tears, including those in the ranks of the clergy. In the background, the choir sang the Doxology.

Bennett and Patricia Thagard came forward, as did Ken and Rachel Reeves. Rachel's eyes were full when she turned away from the bishop; she sobbed after returning to her seat. Robert

Dinkins, a former segregationist, walked up the center aisle with Carolyn. As the queue grew shorter, White announced, "If we've missed you, come on down."

After the congregation exchanged the peace, White stepped to the podium and introduced Bishop Shipps to a standing ovation. "I'm really not used to that kind of welcome," the bishop remarked, genuinely embarrassed. Then, recovering quickly: "I hope the clergy on my left will take note of it." Shipps said the evening was "a happy occasion" for him, and added that it was "an Easter day I will remember more clearly than any other in my life."

When White took the podium again, he ruminated a bit. He said that Church of the King sought "orthodox, creedal Christianity married and blended with the fire and vigor of the Pentecostal experience." He recounted his own Pentecostal roots, his great-great uncle and his grandfather, both Pentecostal preachers. His grandmother was also an Assemblies of God minister. White asked her to stand, one of the newest to be confirmed in the Episcopal Church. White then introduced his father, "Brother Jimmy," and his mother, Ann, also new Episcopalians.

Before the celebration of the Eucharist, Bishop Shipps consecrated the altar, a simple table of white marble that had been the object of considerable interest to members of the Friday evening prayer group. ("That's not at all what I expected," someone had remarked at the time.) During the Sunday morning service Stan White had explained that the altar would be consecrated after the confirmations and before the celebration of the Eucharist that evening. "That doesn't mean you can't touch it or anything like that," he said. "It means only that the altar should be treated with reverence and respect." During that same service, at the conclusion of his extemporaneous homily, White had given an altar call, the script for which came straight out of a Billy Graham crusade. He asked for every head to be bowed and every eye closed. "You don't want to leave this place," he implored, "without knowing that everything is right between you and God." White acknowledged each hand with a simple "yes" and then, as the synthesizer played softly in the background, offered a formula prayer for those seeking salvation. "Dear Jesus, I ask you to forgive me today," White intoned, "cleanse me… wash me in your blood… make me righteous in your eyes."

When it came time to receive Holy Communion— "the memorial of our redemption," in the words of the Book of Common Prayer—the celebrant held up the bread and the wine from the newly consecrated altar and announced "the gifts of God for the people of God." He invited the congregation to "take them in remembrance that Christ died for you, and feed on him in your heart by faith, with thanksgiving."

By the end of the recessional (a reprise of "How Magnificent Is Your Name"), it was 9:30. The memorable service of "Confirmation, Consecration of an Altar, and a Celebration of the Holy Eucharist" had lasted more than two-and-a-half hours. Euphoria had gradually given way to exhaustion. The congregation heaved a kind of collective sigh, and the reception afterward in the rear of the warehouse provided occasion to exchange congratulations and to evaluate the day's events. "If that don't move you, you got to be dead," one parishioner said breathlessly to another. "That's all I got to say."

"I don't think this would go over big in Massachusetts," acknowledged Bishop Harry Shipps, but in the South, with its predominant evangelical ethos, Episcopalians are more attuned to evangelical sympathies. Judging from the overwhelmingly positive response from other bishops, Shipps predicted broad acceptance of Church of the King within Episcopal circles. Although he anticipated that the "problem will be with liberals," he cited the "remarkable unanimity" within the diocese. "I hope this is not an isolated phenomenon," he said. "I'm convinced that the church catholic is going to include both Roman Catholics and Pentecostals—and they're going to be a happy family."

Indeed, the Roman Catholics of Valdosta had weighed in with a large floral bouquet of "prayerful congratulations" to Church of the King. "If anyone had told me years ago that Saint John's Catholic Church would be sending us flowers," Stan White remarked in the morning service, "I never would have believed them." The Pentecostals in town were less forthcoming.

When I asked Stan's father how his erstwhile colleagues in the Assemblies of God would react to the day's events, he shook his head. "I don't know if the Assemblies of God will pay any attention," he said, "but they would probably dismiss it as a lapse into dead orthodoxy."

The din of the fellowship hall began slowly to abate. The congregation, many of them newly rooted within historic Christianity, emerged from the sanctuary into the bracing air of a spring night in Georgia.

Throughout the evening Stan White wore a proud smile, the expression of a father having just announced the birth of his first child. His congregation's pilgrimage from the Pentecostalism of Evangel Assembly of God to the charismatic fervor of Church of the King, rooted in the sacramentalism of the historic church, may have been long and gradual, but it was joyous, and was culminated in sweet and unabashed celebration.

No one, least of all Stan White, had second thoughts about the journey. "I see God's hand now," White says. "I'm almost thankful that the deacons released me. I can look back and see the providence of God."

ABOUT THE AUTHOR

Dr. Ronald E. Cottle has been serving the body of Christ for more than six decades. He has extensive experience in teaching, pastoring, public speaking, education administration and both radio and television.

He has developed more than one hundred advanced courses of Christian development and biblical training and has authored more than one hundred books encompassing ministry, leadership, biblical studies, and church development.

Dr. Cottle's teaching style has been called "scholarship on fire" by those who have attended his lectures. His unique style always contains the compassion of a shepherd, the urgency of a prophet and the wisdom of a statesman.

His thoughts and counsel are straightforward, dynamic, and powerful. His teachings will help today's spiritual leaders and other sincere "thinking Christians" to discover the mystery and the majesty of the Bible.

Dr. Cottle has earned a Bachelor of Arts (A.B.) degree from Florida Southern College, Lakeland, Florida; a Master of Divinity (M.Div.) from Lutheran Theological Seminary, Columbia, South Carolina; and a Doctor of Philosophy (Ph.D.) in Religion from the University of Southern California, Los Angeles. He also earned a Master of Science in Education (M.S.Ed.) and a Doctor of Education (Ed.D.) from U.S.C.

For more information about Dr. Ron Cottle and his numerous books and teachings, go to: www.roncottle.com.

THE COTTLE LIBRARY

Dr. Cottle has worked tirelessly in his home office for the past two decades compiling his five hundred notebooks, fifty plus college courses, fifty plus books, hundreds of sermon outlines, publications, articles, and newsletters. Dr. Cottle and Dr. Thomas Hale are cataloging everything into an online library.

The library contains digital files (PDF and Microsoft Word) available for download, streaming audio files and streaming video files.

Please visit the library at: www.cottlelibrary.com.